My first book of time

Illustrated by Julie Park

Consultant: Peter Patilla

Oxford University Press

8 o'clock

time to have breakfast

9 o'clock

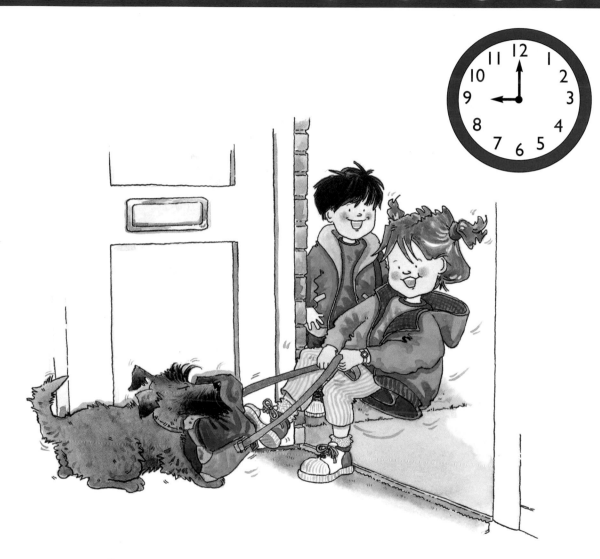

time to go to school

10 o'clock

time to learn

11 o'clock

time to play

12.00

12 o'clock

time to have lunch

PM

1.00

1 o'clock

time to tidy up

2 o'clock

time to go shopping

3 o'clock

time to have a snack

4 o'clock

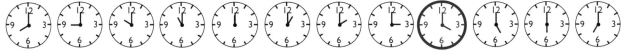

time to go for a walk

PM
5.00

5 o'clock

time to help in the kitchen

6 o'clock

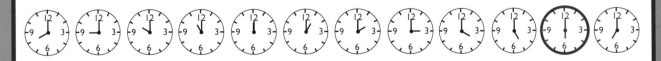

time to have dinner

7 o'clock

time to have a bath

8 o'clock

time to go to bed

What time is it?